LOIRE VALLEY TRAVEL GUIDE FOR WINE LOVERS, CYCLISTS & CASTLE EXPLORERS

Discover France's Fairytale Châteaux, Scenic Vineyards & the Loire à Vélo Trail with Expert Tips for Unforgettable Outdoor Adventures

Copyright © 2025 by Aarav Nath Wayfarer

All rights reserved. No part of this book may be copied, stored, or shared in any form without written permission from the author, except brief quotes for reviews or academic use.

This guide is for personal use only. The author is not liable for any outcomes based on the content.

For permissions or inquiries, contact via the publishing platform.

TABLE OF CONTENT

INTRODUCTION

CHAPTER 1

GREETINGS FROM THE VALLEY OF THE LOIRE

The Loire Valley's Unique Characteristics

Regional Overview: Climate, Culture, and Geography

Wine, Wheels, and Wonder: Why This Guide Is for You

How to Get the Most Adventure Out of This Book

CHAPTER 2

CONFIDENTLY ORGANIZING YOUR LOIRE ADVENTURE

Top Times to Go for Wine, Châteaux, and Cycling

How Much Time Is Actually Needed?

Train Routes, Regional Airports, and Automobile Options

Smart Budgeting: Unexpected Expenses & Local Advice

CHAPTER 3

DECIPHERING THE EXPERIENCE OF THE LOIRE À VÉLO

Loire à Vélo: What Is It? Route Dissection

Typical Itineraries: Where to Begin and Finish

Equipment Guide: Rentals, Bags, and Bikes

Local Cycling Etiquette, Safety, and Navigation

CHAPTER 4

REAL-LIFE FAIRYTALE CASTLE EXPLORATIONS

The Top 10 Châteaux You Must See (and Why)

Undiscovered Treasures Most Travelers Ignore

Guided vs. Self-Guided Castle Tours

How to Act at a Château: What to Do Inside

CHAPTER 5

THE LOIRE WINE LOVER'S JOURNEY

Overview of Wine Regions in the Loire Valley (AOPs)

Winery Tours: Bookings, Samples, and Important Information

Meeting the Winemakers: An Overview of Culture

Purchasing Local Wine and Sending It Home

CHAPTER 6

ACCOMMODATIONS: BUDGET GEMS, CHATEAU HOTELS, AND VINEYARD RETREATS

Unusual Places to Stay: Sleep Among Vines or in a Castle

Inexpensive Choices Along the Way

Reservation Advice for Busiest Times

Local Accommodations vs. Chain Hotels: Benefits and Drawbacks

CHAPTER 7

DELIGHTFUL PIT STOPS EN ROUTE

Customary Recipes to Sample in Every Sub-Region

Top Dining Establishments with a View

Markets, Bakeries, and Cafés: Where Cyclists Refuel

Seasonal Foods & Farmers' Markets

CHAPTER 8

OUTDOOR EXPERIENCES THAT GO BEYOND CYCLING

Loire River Canoeing & Kayaking

Balloon Rides in Hot Air Over Vineyards

Forest Walks & Hiking Trails Close to Castles

Nature Reserves & Locations for Birdwatching

CHAPTER 9

LOCAL LIFE, LANGUAGE HINTS, AND CULTURAL ETIQUETTE

Essential French Words for Passengers

How to Respectfully Engage Locals

Holiday Closures, Strikes, and Opening Hours

Local Customs & Festival Features

CHAPTER 10

INSIGHTFUL TRAVEL ADVICE & COMMON ERRORS TO AVOID

The Top Ten Rookie Errors (and How to Avoid Them)

How to Steer Clear of Tourist Pitfalls

Essentials for Safety, Health, and Travel Insurance

Keeping in Touch: Apps, Wi-Fi, and SIM Cards

CONCLUSION

INTRODUCTION

Have you ever imagined riding a bicycle through beautiful vineyards, enjoying fine wine in cellars that date back centuries, and exploring castles straight out of a fairy tale?

You're right at the right place if that sounds like your ideal getaway. For tourists who want more than simply a list of places to see, the Loire Valley is a profoundly engaging, soul-stirring adventure rather than just another destination on the French map.

This book was written with you in mind—the inquisitive adventurer, the leisurely tourist, the wine enthusiast, the castle fantasizer, the biker who enjoys the ride rather than the final goal. The ideal fusion of outdoor adventure, cultural immersion, and decadent pleasure is probably what you're looking for, whether you're planning your first vacation to France or returning for a more comprehensive experience. You're not here to take in the superficial sights. You want freedom to explore at your own speed, beauty, and sincerity.

And the Loire Valley provides just that. However, this book goes one step farther.

This book is unique because it emphasizes the three essential components of an absolutely remarkable vacation to the Loire Valley:

- **The Castles:** Not just lists, but carefully chosen paths, insider information, and undiscovered treasures.
- **The Wine:** Where to meet actual winemakers, how to taste like a pro, and local vineyards.

- **The Cycling Experience:** Loire à Vélo explained with useful advice rather than merely flowery language.

Every chapter is designed to guide you through the area in a manner that is both very helpful and inspirational. There won't be long history lectures or ambiguous advice. To help you save time, prevent annoyance, and improve your vacation, you will instead get practical, honest advice, itinerary suggestions, logistical assistance, and traveler-tested insights.

You are not supposed to be impressed by this tutorial. Its purpose is to prepare you. You'll discover insider information that only locals and frequent visitors are aware of, such as which castles provide uncrowded views of the dawn, which wine tastings include lunches at the vineyard, and which villages greet bicycles with repair kits and baked tarts. These little but significant nuances are what separate a "nice trip" from a journey you will speak about for years to come.

Inside, you will find:

- The top châteaux to see (and the ones that aren't worth the extra trip)
- How to organize your own trip to the Loire à Vélo without a tour or guide
- Where to get genuine local wine experiences away from tourist buses
- Off-the-beaten-path paths, riverbank marketplaces, and secret settlements that you may otherwise overlook
- How to steer clear of blunders that might ruin your ideal vacation

While many tours attempt to cover too much ground too quickly, this one takes its time so that you may explore the Loire Valley more thoroughly, intelligently, and meaningfully. Instead of being a tourist with wide eyes sifting through pamphlets, you will know precisely how to traverse the area like an experienced traveler.

In fact, this journey is too significant to be left up to chance. You're devoting your time, money, and effort to an area that merits careful consideration. This book guarantees that your days will be full of magic rather than mistakes. Each page was created to provide you a clear idea of what to do, when to do it, and how to maximize every moment as you boldly enter the Loire Valley.

Thus, inhale deeply. You're going to explore one of France's most captivating areas in a manner that most tourists never do. From the peaceful wine alleys to the castles perched on hills, from riverbank cafes to the Loire's most memorable rides, let this book be your traveling companion.

CHAPTER 1

GREETINGS FROM THE VALLEY OF THE LOIRE

What comes to mind when you shut your eyes and see France outside of Paris? The Loire Valley is home to rolling vineyards, turreted castles, peaceful riverbank communities, and peaceful roads dotted with poplar trees. Despite seeming frozen in time, the city is teeming with culture, adventure, and vitality. More significantly, however, it's a place made for adventure-seeking, independent, and inquisitive tourists like you.

This chapter serves as your starting point for learning about the Loire Valley as an experiential trip via history, taste, and the open countryside, rather than merely as a place on a map. You need a firm grasp of what makes this area so exceptional before you start riding your bike through vineyards or touring the imposing châteaux. You should also have a solid understanding of the geography, the weather, and how the deeply ingrained customs and culture influence your stay. Above all, you should understand how this travel guide was created to assist you—not with hurried itineraries or general advice, but with thoughtful, useful advice.

Consider this chapter to be your guide. Your ability to plan a journey that suits your own travel preferences will improve as you get a deeper understanding of the Loire Valley's rhythm, richness, and distinctiveness. Your journey starts here, with information, clarity, and purpose, regardless of whether you're here for the wine, the castles, the bicycle trails, or all three.

The Loire Valley's Unique Characteristics

Perhaps you're wondering: Why the Loire? Why not Provence, Champagne, or Bordeaux? It's a legitimate query. There are many alluring places to visit in France, but the Loire Valley is a special place that combines the greatest aspects of many different worlds in one area.

Let's start by discussing the sceneries. The longest river in France, the Loire, connects ancient cities and quaint villages as it meanders past lush vineyards, wooded woods, and beautiful farmland. There is space to breathe here, in contrast to the congested beaches of the Riviera or the bustling cityscapes of Paris. You may stop at communities that seem to have been spared the effects of contemporary life, ride or drive beside peaceful canals, or have a picnic on the banks of rivers.

Then, there are the châteaux—more than 300, not just one or two. Some are set on slopes or concealed behind rows of vineyards, while others rise majestically from reflected moats. You'll pass through libraries with centuries' worth of history, royal gardens, spiral stairs, and old kitchens. However, many of them are available for investigation and some even provide on-site wine tastings or overnight stays, so they are not museum exhibits that are restricted to visitors.

Another remarkable aspect is the wine culture. This isn't the formality and flamboyant reds of Bordeaux. With light reds from Chinon to sophisticated rosés in Anjou, and dry whites in

Sancerre to sparkling Crémants in Saumur, the Loire Valley offers a more diversified and accessible wine scene. The fact that many of the winemakers you'll encounter are genuine, enthusiastic locals who still individually welcome guests makes it a wine lover's paradise.

The rhythm of the Loire Valley, however, is perhaps its most remarkable characteristic. Here, everything goes a little more slowly. There is no compulsion to see and do everything in a single day, nor is there a hurry. You are urged to remain an additional day in a location that catches your heart, to ride at your own speed, or to linger over a glass of wine. That is uncommon, which is why so many visitors leave the Loire with more than just pictures—they take with them memories that are lasting and intimate.

What, then, is so unique about the Loire Valley? It's more than simply the scenery, wine, or castles. Whether you're a first-time visitor to France or an experienced tourist seeking something more profound, it's the way these components combine to create a place that seems authentic, approachable, and inspiring.

Regional Overview: Climate, Culture, and Geography

Understanding the layout of the Loire Valley and what to anticipate in terms of weather, customs, and local life is essential before you start organizing your travel itineraries and selecting your must-see wineries.

Layout and Geography

Between the city of Orléans in the east and Angers in the west, the Loire Valley spans about 280 kilometers (175 miles) along the middle portion of the Loire River. It encompasses the regional centers of Tours, Blois, Saumur, and Chinon as well as many French departments, including Loiret, Loir-et-Cher, Indre-et-Loire, and Maine-et-Loire.

This indicates that the region is a broad expanse of territory with various subregions, each with its own distinct character, rather than a single, compact area. More rural and wine-focused are the eastern regions around Sancerre. Châteaux and culture abound in central regions such as Amboise and Tours. The western border, close to Saumur and Angers, combines medieval charm, cuisine, and wine.

Planning will be easier if you understand this arrangement. For example, you might choose a home base in one location and take day excursions to explore the surrounding areas, or you could use the well defined Loire à Vélo path to bike from town to town.

Local Life and Cultural Rhythms

The Loire Valley lacks the glitz and bustle of the Côte d'Azur and Paris. Its understatement is what makes it so appealing. Here, people adapt to the seasons and the environment. In the morning, markets are bustling, and by lunchtime, they are calm. Meals are taken slowly. There are significant traditions, particularly in the areas of agriculture, wine, and gastronomy, and many residents take satisfaction in upholding the traditional methods.

You'll see that the hospitality here is genuine rather than commercial. You are treatcd like a friend by winemakers. B&B hosts provide thorough guidance on nearby trails. When chefs come out of the kitchen, they want to know whether you liked your meal. The Loire experience includes these encounters, therefore they are not uncommon.

Additionally, even though tourism is expanding, it hasn't taken over the whole area, so you still have room to explore, stroll, and interact with people without feeling crowded.

Patterns of the Climate and Weather

Although the Loire Valley has a mild, temperate climate, It might be helpful to plan your activities and prepare appropriately if you know what to anticipate in each season.

1. Spring (April–June): A great season to cycle and see blooming gardens. Anticipate warm afternoons and cold mornings. It may rain, but it typically doesn't last long.

2. Summer (July–August): Busiest time of year with dozens of events and more daylight hours. Evening breezes often help to cool things down, although days may grow sweltering, particularly in late July.

3. Fall (September–October): As harvest season starts, this is the perfect time for wine enthusiasts. The scenery becomes rust-red and golden, while the weather stays good.

4. Quiet and atmospheric throughout the winter months of November through March. Prices fall, communities are quiet, and several

châteaux shut. Excellent for intimate wine tastings held inside.

The Loire Valley presents a new image with each season. The secret is to understand how to match your own objectives, such as riding a bike, tasting wine, or seeing a castle, with the actual circumstances.

Wine, Wheels, and Wonder: Why This Guide Is for You

The majority of travel guides, let's face it, either gloss over the Loire Valley or overburden you with material that seems to be written for everyone and no one at the same time. You are the very special sort of traveler—for whom this book was written.

You're the kind of person that seeks out more information. You're not only here to "take in the scenery." To experience them is why you are here. Instead of merely reading a tasting note, you want to sample the wine where it's produced. Instead of merely driving from monument to monument, you want to cycle a woodland track that finishes in a medieval village square. Instead of merely taking pictures from the parking lot, you want to be able to stroll into the castles.

That attitude is immediately addressed in this handbook.

1. Those that like wine: You may get easily comprehensible information on the area wine regions, including Vouvray, Chinon, and Sancerre. It won't only list grapes and labels, however. You'll discover how to handle a tasting, where to meet small producers, how to stay away from tourist attractions, and how to transport bottles home without any problems.

2. Riding bicycles: This book provides all the information you need, including recommended itineraries, gear suggestions, route insights, and pit breaks along the way, regardless of your level of riding expertise or your desire to enjoy the Loire à Vélo path.

3. Explorers of Castle: Not all châteaux are made equal. Whether you're a history buff, art lover, gardener, or a parent, this guide helps you choose the ones that best suit your interests. Additionally, you will get useful information such as the ideal locations for photos, opening hours, and which ones are worth your time (and which aren't).

Additionally, this book is brimming with local knowledge that you would only learn via insider chats or return trips. The type of information that isn't found on the first page of a Google search or in the brochure of a tourist board. Written for real-world travelers, this book is about real-world experience.

How to Get the Most Adventure Out of This Book

You don't read this book once and put it away. It's a tool—a reference you'll use as your preparation progresses, as your itinerary changes, and even when you make adjustments depending on the weather, your energy level, or your curiosity.

To get the most out of it, follow these steps:

1. Go Deep After Starting Broad: Start with the planning, regions, and highlights chapters.

After deciding on a focus (cycling, wine, castles, or all three), explore the corresponding areas.

2. Make use of the checklists and advice: Rather than only providing explanations, each main part offers really helpful suggestions. To go from concept to action, look for route breakdowns, seasonal insights, and packed advice.

3. Combine and Combine: Your journey doesn't have to be linear, just as the Loire Valley isn't. Create a personalized itinerary using this book. Do you want to ride a bike between castles and explore two wine regions? What you need to make that smooth will be found.

4. Use It While Traveling: This book offers resources to help you adapt while on the trip, such as emergency contacts, weather forecasting, and advice on local manners. Have a print or digital copy on hand.

Ultimately, this book was intended to be useful, adaptable, and motivating. It will not only direct your travels but also mold your viewpoint, enabling you to see the Loire Valley as more than simply a location; rather, it will be a profoundly unforgettable experience that you have crafted for yourself.

CHAPTER 2

CONFIDENTLY ORGANIZING YOUR LOIRE ADVENTURE

Only if you arrange your trip with open minds will traveling through the Loire Valley seem like entering a dream. The area is friendly, serene, and very rewarding, but it's not one of those locations where you simply "wing." Because of its many tiny villages, dispersed châteaux, seasonal variations, and peculiarities in transportation, you'll need to carefully consider how much time you have, how you'll travel about, and how to balance everything from the weather to your budget.

Giving you confidence in the choices you'll need to make before you ever set foot in France is the goal of this chapter, not simply in the practical aspects. I'll explain the ideal times to travel based on your objectives, assist you in determining how long to stay, take you through your possibilities for transportation, and break down the sometimes disregarded expenses that may have an impact on your vacation. Whether you're a small group seeing castles and rural charm, a couple on a wine excursion, or a lone biker, you'll leave with a plan that suits your travel style.

You'll be able to plan your Loire adventure clearly by the conclusion of this chapter, steer clear of beginner blunders, and have flexibility to adapt, breathe, and explore at your own pace.

Top Times to Go for Wine, Châteaux, and Cycling

One of the best choices you can make is to plan your vacation appropriately. Every season in the Loire Valley has its own distinct personality; some are better for wine tasting, others for cycling, and some for touring castles. You can find bike lanes muddy, vineyards closed, or castles undergoing renovations if you come at the incorrect season for your objectives.

For good reason, many tourists prefer the spring (April to early June) season. The air is clean, the countryside is in blossom, and the cities and highways are not yet crowded. With cold mornings, pleasant afternoons, and no rain, this is also the time of year when bikers enjoy the finest weather for lengthy rides. Picnics, lengthy outdoor meals by the river, and

Loire à Vélo rides are all great springtime activities if you're looking for beauty and action.

The peak season is Summer (mid-June through August). Longer days, lively marketplaces, and a few festivals in almost every town are to be expected. But summertime may be crowded, particularly in the more well-known château towns of Chenonceau, Blois, and Amboise. Prices increase, lodgings fill up fast, and roads get congested. However, if you can tolerate the warmer days and are prepared to make reservations in advance, this is the time of year when the area is most vibrant.

For wine enthusiasts, fall (September to mid-October) is perfect. Harvest season is upon us. The vineyards gleam with rich reds and golds, and you'll see winemakers at their best. During this season, a lot of wineries have special harvest parties, tastings, and tours. Even if the daylight hours are becoming shorter and the mornings might be chilly, cycling is still enjoyable. The vibe of the area changes, becoming more local and less touristic.

A distinct tale is told throughout Winter (mid-October through March). Some castles cut down on their hours or shut. Tours may not be available at vineyards. Trails for cycling might be icy and slippery. However, there are benefits. Prices decrease. There are still cities like Tours and Angers. There are wine bars bustling with locals and warm eateries with fires. Winter could be a good option if you're not interested in outdoor activities and would rather have a quiet, cultural escape.

To choose the best moment, consider the following: Do you like bustling energy or peaceful roads? Which would you prefer: quaint tasting rooms or sunny vineyards? Would you accept reduced costs in exchange for milder temperatures? Your response should inform not only the dates you choose, but also the structure of your whole itinerary.

How Much Time Is Actually Needed?

There is always more to see in the Loire Valley, even if you spend two weeks there. However, two weeks is not enough time to plan a rich, satisfying journey. A realistic plan that fits your travel style and a clear idea of what you want to experience are what you do need.

It will take more days to cycle the Loire à Vélo than it would to drive. If wine tasting is your main goal, you may set up shop in a key wine area and go on day visits. You should group trips in certain zones if you're visiting many châteaux.

Let's dissect this.

3–4 Days

One base, such as Amboise or Saumur, and one main topic should be the focus of a brief visit. With three or four trips, you may complete a château sampler or dedicate all of your time to wine and cuisine in a particular area, such as Chinon. Stay in places with easy access and limit your riding to a small section of the Loire à Vélo. First-timers who wish to sample without hurrying will love this duration.

5–7 Days

You're speaking now. You may experiment with many themes in a week without becoming burned out. For instance, ride to Chinon and spend a few more days in the wine region after spending a couple of days in Tours seeing châteaux and local markets. You may take your time—cycling one day, wine tasting the next, and then castle-hopping—but you still have time to relax and take it all in throughout a whole week.

10–14 Days

If you want to accomplish everything and do it well, this is the perfect length. You may visit the royal castles at Blois and Chambord, take wine excursions in Saumur and Chinon, and ride the Loire à Vélo for extended periods of time without feeling rushed if you have this much time. Additionally, you may eat at slower restaurants, spend more time in lesser-known areas, and go to weekend markets or local activities.

Your energy level, priorities, and desired amount of travel between destinations should all be taken into consideration when choosing the number of days. Whether you want to pack every day or allow time for exploration, this advice will help you create a schedule that works for you.

Train Routes, Regional Airports, and Automobile Options

If you prepare in advance, traveling to and from the Loire Valley may be easy. Regional airports, picturesque local roads, and high-speed trains all provide excellent connections to the area.

However, the kind of travel you're planning should determine how you navigate it.

First, let's examine your arrival choices.

Flying in:

- Paris Charles de Gaulle Airport (CDG) is the nearest major international airport. From there, it takes 1.5 to 2 hours to go to Tours or Angers by direct high-speed rail (TGV).
- Some passengers, particularly those beginning their journey in the western Loire, prefer to fly into Nantes Atlantique Airport. Saumur or Angers are readily accessible by rail or automobile from Nantes.
- Tours Val de Loire Airport is a tiny but handy airport for low-cost flights from

places like London or Dublin or short regional trips.

When you arrive in the area, you must choose between: train, vehicle, or bike? A lot of tourists combine all three.

By Train:

The rail system in France is dependable and quick. You may swiftly travel from Paris to important cities like Tours, Angers, or Orléans with the TGV (Train à Grande Vitesse). From there, smaller towns including Blois, Amboise, Saumur, and Chinon are connected by local TER trains.

For day travels between castles or for short excursions while staying in one town, trains are perfect. Many of the routes, particularly those along the Loire à Vélo, are also bike-friendly.

By Automobile:

You have the most flexibility when you go by automobile, particularly whether you're visiting secret towns, tiny vineyards, or distant châteaux. Compared to France's major cities, driving here is more laid back and the roads are beautiful and well-maintained.

In Tours, Angers, or even Paris, you may rent a vehicle. Just keep in mind that automatic vehicles are less common in France, so if you're uncomfortable with a manual gearbox, make your reservation as soon as possible. Additionally, if you want to drive, it's recommended looking for lodgings with on-site parking since some cities have small streets or little parking.

By bicycle:

You are in one of the most bike-friendly areas in Europe if you are a cyclist. The 900-kilometer Loire à Vélo trail winds through vineyards, woodlands, and riverbank villages, among other types of terrain. To assist you travel light, several towns provide luggage transfer services or bike rental stations.

While some tourists choose to bike the whole journey, others select a section and mix it with rail travel. In any case, preparing your speed and route ahead of time can help you steer clear of lengthy, exhausting sections or unsupported routes.

Ultimately, your mobility strategy should align with your travel objectives. Trains are an excellent option for châteaux in small spaces. Cars provide you more alternatives in wine country. The bike is the best for full immersion and gradual travel.

Smart Budgeting: Unexpected Expenses & Local Advice

Compared to Paris or the French Riviera, the Loire Valley isn't particularly costly, but if you don't prepare ahead, it may be quite expensive. The goal of this section is to help you make smart choices so that you may spend more on the things that are important to you and not waste all of your money on things that aren't.

Lodging:

Costs vary greatly. A mid-range hotel room may cost €90 to €160 per night at the busiest times of the year, while quaint B&Bs (chambres d'hôtes) often cost €70 to €110. Better prices may be secured by making reservations in advance, particularly if you're going in June, July, or September. Smaller towns sometimes provide cheaper rates than the well-known château cities if you're on a tight budget.

Movement:

- Train fares are generally reasonable, but if you book at the last minute, high-speed trains (TGV) may cost more than you anticipated. For greatest savings, always make reservations in advance.
- The cost of renting a car varies based on the kind of transmission and the place of

pickup. Keep in mind that some castle lots have daily costs, so account for fuel, tolls, and parking.
- Cycling is reasonably priced, but compare prices if you want to hire cycles for a week or longer. Some services, like luggage transfers, save you a lot of trouble but come at an additional expense.

Castle Visits:

The cost of admission to châteaux varies from €8 to €15 per site. That may increase if you include audio guides, guided tours, or unique displays. Some castles offer discount passes or combined tickets for many visits. Before you travel, do some research on that. Additionally, keep in mind that not all castles accept credit cards at the gate, so be prepared with cash.

Wine tastings:

Not all tastings are complimentary. €5–€10 per tasting may be charged by larger, more commercial vineyards, particularly if food is served. Free samples may be provided by small producers, but if you like the wine, you're likely to purchase a bottle or two. The cost of shipping wine home may quickly pile up, particularly when taxes or insurance are involved.

Meals & Dining:

A three-course meal with wine may cost €30 to €50 per person, while a lunch at a casual café may cost €12 to €18. Bakeries and markets are excellent places to save money. You may feast like a king or queen by the river and easily have a picnic for less than €10.

Other Unexpected Expenses:

- ATM costs for foreign cards
- Access to public restrooms in certain towns
- Gratuities for tour drivers or local guides (little tips are appreciated for good service, but not expected in France)
- SIM cards or data plans if you're traveling without Wi-Fi

You may create a budget that represents your priorities with careful preparation and realistic expectations, whether that means indulging in a stay at a castle, going to wine tastings every night, or just traveling worry-free.

CHAPTER 3

DECIPHERING THE EXPERIENCE OF THE LOIRE À VÉLO

The Loire à Vélo is your invitation to a living postcard if you've ever imagined riding a bicycle past picturesque French towns, riverbank vineyards, brilliant sunflower fields, and castles straight out of a fairy tale. This chapter serves as your guide to comprehending, organizing, and succeeding on one of the most popular long-distance cycling trips in Europe. Regardless of your level of experience, this area will provide you with the useful resources, insider information, and route expertise you need to feel secure and enthusiastic about traveling on two wheels.

Beyond practicalities, however, I'll help you understand what it's like to ride a bike rather than take a tour bus to a château, drink wine under a 16th-century archway, or cruise along peaceful rural roads. You'll discover the Loire Valley's true pace, which is leisurely, picturesque, and very fulfilling.

Let's dissect the Loire à Vélo as a living experience that will alter your perspective on travel, connections, and France, rather than as a chart of kilometers and trail markers.

Loire à Vélo: What Is It? Route Dissection

Following the Loire River from the Atlantic coast at Saint-Nazaire to the town of Nevers in central France, the Loire à Vélo is a designated cycling route that is around 900 kilometers (560 miles) long. Don't worry, however; unless you're on a really important long-distance trip, you won't be forced to ride it all. The majority of tourists choose a portion of the route, often between Angers and Orléans, which is home to several of the most famous sites in the area.

Although the whole route is a part of the wider EuroVelo 6, which connects the Atlantic and Black Sea, the Loire portion is unquestionably the most picturesque and accessible. The riverbanks are lined by mostly level, well-kept bike routes that are often kept clear of vehicles. And in the process? Fairy tale-inspired châteaux, rustic wine cellars, outdoor marketplaces, ancient villages, and idyllic fields for a picnic.

You may choose the stretch that best suits your time, endurance, and travel objectives by using the section-by-section analysis provided in this part. For instance:

1. Nantes to Angers: Perfect for relaxing by the river and introducing them to the local culture. Excellent if you're arriving in Nantes via plane.

2. Angers to Saumur: This area is teeming with tuffeau wine caves and vines, so wine enthusiasts delight.

3. Saumur to Tours: Ideal for those who are interested in castles. You'll go by Langeais, Villandry, and Chinon.

4. Tours to Blois: Contains Amboise and the well-known Château de Chenonceau (a short diversion).

5. Blois to Orléans: Blends private villages, wild woodland paths, and regal heritage.

Follow your interests rather than simply the kilometers since every portion has its own atmosphere. This section will assist you in selecting the region in the Loire à Vélo that best suits your ideal vacation, whether your interests are wine, castles, or the countryside.

Typical Itineraries: Where to Begin and Finish

To really enjoy the experience, you don't have to ride the whole journey. Actually, the majority of tourists choose a manageable 3- to 7-day window that is jam-packed with attractions. Whether it's castles, wine, gastronomy, or transportation convenience, I'll explain how to customize your trip in this area.

Here are three completely comprehensive example itineraries:

1. The Traditional 4- to 5-Day Châteaux Loop

- **Beginning:** Tours
- **Finishing:** Blois
- **Reason:** There are several châteaux and wine villages in this area. Consider wine tastings at Montlouis, Amboise, Château de Chenonceau, and cafés along the river.

2. The 3- to 4-day Wine & Vine Escape

- **Beginning:** Saumur
- **Final:** Chinon
- **Reason:** Perfect for wine and cuisine enthusiasts. With plenty of picturesque vineyard vistas, stop at Saumur for sparkling wine and Chinon for reds.

3. The 7–8-Day One-Week Explorer

- **Beginning:** Anger
- **Final:** Orléans

- **Reason:** Castles, towns, caverns, and other gastronomic pleasures are all covered in detail.

Every itinerary includes places that are conveniently accessible by rail, making it simple to go to and from your starting and ending points. Along with the typical daily bike lengths and must-see diversions (such as how to work at Château de Chambord without adding too much time), I also provide advice on where to stay.

This chapter makes sure your trip on the Loire à Vélo is smooth, picturesque, and appropriate for your pace of travel, regardless of how many days you have.

Equipment Guide: Rentals, Bags, and Bikes

To appreciate the Loire à Vélo, you don't have to be an avid cyclist with carbon fiber aspirations. However, understanding what to anticipate and selecting the appropriate equipment may make or ruin your vacation.

I've broken out this portion so you don't have to guess:

1. Selecting Your Bicycle

- Is it better to hire an e-bike, a hybrid, or bring your own? I go over the benefits and drawbacks of each.
- Rental touring bikes are generally accessible and ideal for the mostly level terrain.

- If you want to go further without exerting yourself, e-bikes are a fantastic choice.

2. Packing List

- A detailed equipment list will be provided, which includes panniers, repair kits, information on helmet regulations (children in France are required to wear helmets), and advice on how to dress for weather variations.
- Necessities such as reusable water bottles that attach on your bike, waterproof coverings, and sunscreen.

3. Where to Rent and How to Do It

- In important start towns like Tours, Saumur, and Orléans, I provide you with a

carefully chosen list of reliable rental stores.
- Additionally, information on one-way bike rental services will be provided, saving you the trouble of going back merely to return your equipment.
- Depending on the bike and configuration, prices might vary from €12 to €25 per day.

4. Logistics of Accommodations

- Find "Accueil Vélo" approved accommodations that welcome cyclists, providing safe bike storage, tools, laundry, and sometimes packed meals.

In summary, although it's not necessary to overthink your setup, a little planning can help you avoid last-minute anxiety, pain, and wasted time. I'll assist you in strategically preparing so that you may keep your attention on the road rather than the repair stand.

Local Cycling Etiquette, Safety, and Navigation

Confidence and safety go hand in hand. This paragraph guarantees that you not only enjoy the voyage but also do it in a courteous, law-abiding, and seamless manner.

1. Effective Navigation Tools

- Although the Loire à Vélo route is well defined, I'll demonstrate how to use internet resources like Komoot and Maps.me with local print maps that are accessible at tourist offices.
- How to get maps offline in areas with poor signal strength.

2. Traffic Regulations

- When sharing roads in France, bicycles must abide by ordinary traffic regulations and ride on the right.
- Although they are not required, helmets are strongly advised for adults.
- I'll go over how roundabouts should be handled, when to yield, and how bike lanes differ in urban and rural settings.

3. Hazards & Weather

- Although the Loire Valley is normally safe, you may be surprised by unexpected rain, high gusts along riverbanks, or sloppy mud after storms. I'll assist you in preparing for and managing these circumstances in a composed manner.

4. Handling Emergencies or Flat Tires

- How to utilize emergency lines (112), signal assistance in rural regions, and speak to people in rudimentary French in the event of an emergency.
- I promise you'll be happy to have this breakdown kit checklist.

5. Tips for Cycling Culture

- Do you want to fit in? A simple "Bonjour" or nod to other bikers makes a big difference.
- On shared roadways, don't ride more than two-abreast.

- In busy town centers, always give way to people and get off your horse.

Knowing this will help you become more than simply a tourist; it will help you fit in with the flow of life in the Loire Valley. This portion makes sure that your trip is not only easy but also courteous, profoundly linked, and full of impromptu moments that you will cherish long after the voyage is finished.

CHAPTER 4

REAL-LIFE FAIRYTALE CASTLE EXPLORATIONS

The Loire Valley is known as "the Garden of France" for a reason, but what really makes it seem like something out of a fairy tale are the châteaux, or castles. The heart of the area is made up of these magnificent estates, some of which are royal and lavish and others that are discreetly hidden behind roads lined with trees. This chapter is for you if you've ever imagined riding a bicycle down a river to an ivy-covered tower, drinking wine under the shade of a Renaissance turret, or strolling through rooms previously adorned by monarchs.

You deserve more than a list of tourist sites if you're a traveler who is interested in culture, history, and beauty. There is more to this guide than meets the eye. Here, you'll discover not only the most well-known castles but also the lesser-known ones that most visitors overlook. It will teach you how to experience castle visits in a manner that makes the past come to life without feeling overcrowded, hurried, or disoriented.

This chapter will enable you to enter the narrative and experience the legend, whether you're riding a bicycle along the Loire à Vélo route, organizing a family outing, or enjoying a peaceful time by yourself in a sunlit château garden.

The Top 10 Châteaux You Must See (and Why)

Let's begin with those that you just must see. These are the main players, the Loire Valley's symbols; each has a backstory, a distinctive architectural design, and memorable experiences. I'll explain to you why they are important and how to appreciate them without being swept up in the tourist horde, however, rather than merely listing them.

1. The Château de Chambord

It's bold, large, and impossible to ignore. The architecture of Chambord, the biggest château in the Loire, is utterly unique. Its double-helix staircase, which was partially designed by Leonardo da Vinci (yes, that da Vinci), is a design wonder. You tour Chambord from roofs to royal apartments; you don't simply go there. My advice? Don't miss the views from the rooftop patio, and arrive early.

2. The Chenonceau Palace

Chenonceau, which crosses the River Cher like something from a fantasy book, is known as the "Ladies' Château" because of its strong female inhabitants. Its grounds are gorgeous throughout the year, and it is charming and symmetrical. The woodland trails leading up to Chenonceau are like stepping into a dream for riders.

3. The Villandry Castle

Really, come for the gardens. The geometric Renaissance gardens are the main attraction, even if the castle itself is beautiful. From love and music to war and peace, every little element conveys a tale. When everything is in bloom, visit in the late spring or summer.

4. The Château d'Amboise

This old royal home, perched high above the Loire, provides both history and expansive vistas. It also serves as Leonardo da Vinci's ultimate resting place; his adjacent house, Clos Lucé, is also a must-see. Admire the magnificence as you stroll around the ramparts.

5. The Château de Chaumont-sur-Loire

Chaumont, which is less crowded and quite attractive, has an International Garden Festival every year that features cutting-edge floral displays. This is for you if you like nature, art, and castles with a unique twist.

6. Azay-le-Rideau Château

This little château, floating on its own mirrored moat, is a photographer's paradise. It's romantic, easy to handle, and perfect for anyone who desires a more relaxed vacation without compromising style.

7. Saumur Castle

Saumur is as much about the location as the building, with a view over the town and the Loire River. It has a distinct personality and a history connected to military training and equestrian art.

8. The Palace of Blois

This château, which combines Gothic, Renaissance, and Classical architectural elements, is like a live architecture class. It has legends carved into every stone and was once the residence of seven kings and ten queens. The spiral staircase in the Francis I wing is a sight to see.

9. Brézé Château

The surprise? It's mostly subterranean. Explore the network of tunnels, wine cellars, and troglodyte rooms at Brézé, which boasts one of Europe's deepest dry moats. It's immersive, different, and not often visited by tourists.

10. The Langeais Château

With its intricate interior reconstructions and defended towers, this one provides a more thorough look into medieval life. Despite being smaller and less crowded than others, it is packed with historical interest, particularly the chamber where Anne of Brittany and Charles VIII's marriage altered the trajectory of French history.

Undiscovered Treasures Most Travelers Ignore

Let's now depart off the main route. Smaller, less well-known châteaux dotting the Loire Valley provide charm, intimacy, and sometimes no crowds. For tourists seeking genuine experiences away from the large bus crowds, these are ideal.

1. The Château de la Bussière

This charming castle, called the "Fisherman's Château," is dedicated to the history of freshwater fishing. It's perfect if you're traveling with children because of the lovely surroundings and the welcoming atmosphere.

2. Montpoupon Château

Almost like a hidden garden, this secluded château is tucked away in the woods close to Loches. In addition to having a superb museum of hunting and equestrian customs, the interiors have been exquisitely kept.

3. Giezeux Castle

There are many family tales to be told about this privately held château. You may witness restored paintings, antique kitchens, and children's rooms on a private tour with a family descendent.

4. The Château du Rivau

Imagine fantasy and fairy tales. Rivau combines quirky art pieces, themed gardens, and medieval architecture. This is the kind of château that will pique your interest.

5. Talcy Château

Unaffected by the overtourism of more well-known locations, Talcy is a literary gem. Its surviving interiors from the 16th century and lyrical linkages are a silent joy.

These undiscovered treasures are often accessible on a whim and without prior reservation. From the main Loire à Vélo path, they also form great cycling excursions.

Guided vs. Self-Guided Castle Tours

Choosing whether to go on the tour or go it alone is one of the major choices you'll have to make at each château. Here are some tips for choosing what suits your style.

Group or Private Guided Tours

These may provide behind-the-scenes access and often go further into historical history. Some castles charge extra for this, while others include it in the admission price. Guided is the best option if you're interested in history or want a background. In addition, you will have the opportunity to ask questions and learn about the politics and peculiarities of what you are seeing.

Independent Tours

Excellent for adaptability. You are free to take your time, stay where you want to, and skip the parts that don't pique your interest. The majority of châteaux include audio guides (bring headphones) or English guidebooks. Self-guided travel allows you greater flexibility to proceed at your children's own speed.

Guides for Selecting:

- Begin with a guided tour to become acquainted if this is your first time visiting a castle throughout the trip.
- To prevent your weariness, use a self-guided approach on your second or third visit.
- A formal tour may not be as entertaining as interactive exhibitions at the château.

How to Act at a Château: What to Do Inside

What am I supposed to do in a French château, you ask? There are certain written and unwritten norms that assist you make the most of your stay while showing respect for the area, but you don't have to feel scared.

1. Dress comfortably yet with dignity.

Although you don't have to dress up, stay away from attire that is too skimpy or beachwear-like, particularly in locations with chapels or formal salons. Even in the summer, internal temperatures might drop, so pack layers.

2. Different Rules for Photography

While some châteaux completely prohibit photography inside, others permit it with no light. Before taking a picture, always be sure to check the signs or ask the personnel. Generally speaking, taking pictures outside is OK.

3. Pay Attention to Noise

The interiors of many castles are surprisingly silent. There may be nearby tour groups and echoes. Silence your phone and have gentle chats.

4. Keep your hands off the furniture

Unless otherwise indicated, presume it's hands-off, even if you see cozy velvet seats or vintage writing desks. Here, historic preservation is taken very seriously.

5. Be mindful of closing times

Staff may start escorting people out 15 to 30 minutes before the official hour, since many châteaux shut abruptly. Make a plan for your visit to avoid being hurried at the conclusion.

6. Don't bring snacks inside; instead, bring water

Drinking water is okay, particularly during the sweltering summer months, but eating inside is strictly prohibited. Don't bring the picnic to the château gardens or other approved locations.

7. It's Encouraged to Ask Questions

Despite their professional appearance, French employees value sincere attention. Don't be afraid to ask questions; many people can speak English or will locate someone who can.

By following these suggestions, you'll have a more seamless and fulfilling experience and depart from each château with a stronger sense of connection—not just as a visitor, but as a transient visitor to its past.

CHAPTER 5

THE LOIRE WINE LOVER'S JOURNEY

The Loire Valley attracts wine enthusiasts from all over the globe for a reason. This area, which spans over 600 miles of vineyards, historic stone towns, and riverbanks, is more than simply a picturesque area; it is a living, breathing wine map of France. You're not reading a wine list as you read this chapter; rather, you're entering a centuries-old wine culture where vines still grow alongside castles and local vintners welcome guests like members of their family.

This chapter serves as your handy guide to the rich and varied wine culture of the Loire. You'll find clear instructions here whether you're a serious collector, a casual wine enthusiast, or someone who's simply interested in learning more about the origins of Sauvignon Blanc. You'll discover how to politely and confidently engage with winemakers, how to traverse the major wine appellations (AOPs), and what to anticipate when you enter a vineyard. This chapter is full of practical tips based on local knowledge, so when you go to your first taste, you won't feel alienated.

To appreciate the wines of the Loire, you don't have to be a sommelier. However, you can significantly enhance your experience by being aware of a few essentials, such as how to schedule tastings, what to ask, and what to anticipate on a tour. Logistics are covered in this part as well, from organizing sampling itineraries to safely transporting wine home. This area's way of life is intertwined with wine, and you're going to see how it all comes together.

Overview of Wine Regions in the Loire Valley (AOPs)

Understanding the Loire's AOPs (Appellations d'Origine Protégée), each of which has its unique grape varietals, climates, and winemaking traditions, is essential if you're serious about tasting its wines. Here, you're experiencing terroir, location by place, rather than simply "French wine."

The main regions that produce wine are broken out in this section:

- Anjou-Saumur (excellent for Chenin Blanc and sparkling wines)

- Touraine (home of famous names like Vouvray and Chinon),
- Nantes (home of Muscadet, which goes well with oysters), and
- Centre-Loire (Sancerre and Pouilly-Fumé for classic Sauvignon Blancs).

You will discover how the land, microclimates, and the Loire River have influenced each area. This isn't wine snobbery; rather, it's a straightforward, approachable explanation of how to relate your taste to your location. The places that are most suited for tastings, the AOPs that are more walk-in friendly, and the ones that may need more preparation are all recommended for each wine area.

Additionally, you'll learn which varieties are most popular in each area, what local cuisine they go well with, and how they represent the culture of the people who grow them. After reading this section, you'll know what to anticipate when you encounter labels that read "Menetou-Salon" or "Saumur-Champigny."

Winery Tours: Bookings, Samples, and Important Information

Many Loire wineries are family-run, unlike those in Napa or Tuscany, and sometimes do not have full-time personnel for tastings. While some accept impromptu visits, others demand reservations. This section explains how to handle it politely so you don't come up without permission or, worse, while everyone is closed for lunch.

Here are some useful pointers:

- The optimum time of day for a tasting

- What to dress (smart casual is always appropriate)
- How long tastings typically last (generally 30 to 60 minutes)
- How to email or call ahead in easy French (with useful words)
- What type of fee—if any—you should anticipate are all covered.

More significantly, you'll discover how to enter the tasting room not as a hurried tourist but as a considerate visitor. This entails listening when the winemaker shares the history of that rosé with you, asking questions without scrutinizing them, and sipping rather than gulping.

We'll also cover topics you may not know to inquire about: What should you do if you don't like wine? Is it better to swallow or spit? Are kids allowed? Can you then drive? To help you choose your experiences carefully, you will also get an explanation of the distinctions between domaines (private estate producers) and caveau de dégustation (tasting room).

Meeting the Winemakers: An Overview of Culture

Spending time with a winemaker in their own region is one of the most fulfilling experiences you can have in the Loire. Although many producers are eager, inquisitive, and happy to share their work, they also value guests who arrive with basic civility and interest.

This section explores basic manners and cultural understanding while interacting with winemakers:

- When it's OK to snap pictures
- How to appropriately welcome them
- If a present is suitable (which it occasionally is)
- How to express gratitude without going overboard.

You'll discover how to have real conversations even if your French isn't very good. You just need to be kind and kind; fluency is not required. And you could just receive a behind-the-scenes look that others don't get if you really show interest in their products or method.

You'll also learn about local traditions, such as why harvest preparation slows down in August and how many winemakers live just above or next to their cellars. You may better schedule your trips and establish a deeper connection with the people who contribute to the uniqueness of this wine area if you are aware of the rhythm of vineyard life.

Purchasing Local Wine and Sending It Home

Let's now discuss logistics. During your trip, you will likely want to bring a couple (or more) bottles home since you will taste some wines that will stick in your memory. However, how can it be accomplished without going over budget or using too many bottles?

This section demonstrates how to purchase wisely:

- Things to consider when purchasing directly from the vineyard as opposed to a nearby wine store,

- What your airline will (and won't) accept in checked luggage
- How to check for export-ready packaging
- How to ship wine internationally without getting caught in customs difficulties.

Additionally, you'll discover useful tools like:

- The best local wine carriers in places like Tours, Saumur, and Angers
- Bottle limitations for non-EU visitors
- Advice on how to bargain for better prices on larger purchases
- Advice on how to store wine carefully while traveling so that it remains in optimal condition when returning home.

We'll also discuss which wines are the simplest to locate back home (so you don't have to bring them) and which brands and vintages to prioritize if you're limited on baggage space. By following this approach, you can steer clear of beginner blunders like leaving that priceless bottle of wine in the vehicle to bake or purchasing unpasteurized wine that isn't exportable.

By the end of this segment, you will know how to purchase sensibly, taste with confidence, and take home not only memories but also the tale of each vineyard from the Loire.

CHAPTER 6

ACCOMMODATIONS: BUDGET GEMS, CHATEAU HOTELS, AND VINEYARD RETREATS

Your trip to the Loire Valley might be totally changed by the lodging you choose. In addition to finding a bed, you're creating memories, strengthening your ties to the area, and providing yourself with time to relax, think, and enjoy the rhythm of life in the verdant heartland of France. This chapter has you covered whether your desire is to stretch your budget over many nights without compromising charm, to stroll under historic beams in a centuries-old château, or to wake up to fields of grapes right outside your window.

The hospitality of the Loire Valley is abundant. The combination of upscale château hotels with opulent gardens and wine cellars, rustic vineyard guesthouses that provide hands-on harvest experiences, chic B&Bs nestled within quiet towns, and dependable, reasonably priced accommodations perfect for longer stays or bikers is what makes it special. Your choice of lodging affects how you see the scenery, the wine culture, and even how easily you can get to the main roads and points of interest.

A comprehensive overview of your lodging possibilities, customized to your preferred travel style, is provided in this chapter. Perhaps you're seeking a romantic indulgence, a useful rest area for cyclists, or a place that brings you near to the vineyards and the outdoors. Additionally, you will get useful advice on how to make wise reservations, locate hidden treasures in the area, and choose whether to go big or cut down depending on your trip schedule. Make good use of this accommodation plan.

Unusual Places to Stay: Sleep Among Vines or in a Castle

Staying someplace that has a tale to tell has a really enchanting quality. Sleeping in a centuries-old château that was previously inhabited by aristocracy or staying at a vineyard retreat where you can see dewy grapevines reaching over undulating hills in the morning are common options in the Loire. These aren't fantastical concepts. They are incredibly bookable and quite authentic.

Consider château hotels if luxury is your goal. With a focus on comfort and style, many have been refurbished to provide private tastings, fine dining, and historic charm. Some even operate their own on-site wineries. Anticipate historical furniture, canopy beds, exposed beams, and gardens that you can really explore.

Vineyard guesthouses are a great option for anyone seeking something more private and grounded. They allow you to experience the rhythms of vineyard life and are often family-run. Nearly all hosts provide peaceful, lovely settings away from the bustle of the city, while some provide home-cooked dinners and others give you a tour of their wine cellars.

Depending on the time of year and the quality of service, these stays might cost anywhere from €120 to €400+ each night. Consider farm lodgings (gîtes) for a less upscale but equally atmospheric experience. These are excellent for longer visits and often include kitchens, which makes cooking with ingredients from the local market simple.

These unique sites fill up quickly, particularly in the spring and early autumn, so make your reservation early. Don't just depend on international platforms. The greatest château or vineyard stays may be found on French-specific booking websites or by getting in touch with the host directly via email or their website.

Inexpensive Choices Along the Way

To get a good night's sleep in the Loire Valley, you don't have to spend a lot. In fact, the most memorable stays are often the most straightforward. Every major town along the Loire à Vélo route offers good alternatives for those on a limited budget or riding the route—consider Tours, Amboise, Saumur, Blois, and Angers.

Low-cost hotels, guesthouses, and bed and breakfasts may be found for between €60 and €100 per night, with breakfast often included. The hosts are generally quite helpful when it comes to food ideas, bike shortcuts, and local insights. These are often family-run establishments.

Some of the smaller communities also have community gîtes and youth hostels. These are particularly helpful if you're riding a bike for a long time and all you need is a clean bed and a warm shower. Most provide a hearty meal in the morning along with safe bike storage.

Another inexpensive option is to camp, particularly if you like being outside. Along the Loire, campgrounds are often well-kept, situated in picturesque areas along the river, and include tent sites as well as tiny cottages or mobile homes.

Use websites run by municipal tourist offices, Gîtes de France, or online booking services like Booking.com and Airbnb to make reservations for these stays. Look via area networks such as Accueil Vélo or Loire à Vélo partners for hostels and shared accommodations.

Reservation Advice for Busiest Times

Spring (April to June) and autumn harvest (September to mid-October) are the two primary peak seasons in the Loire Valley. Your options for accommodations may quickly narrow if you're traveling during these months. It's essential to plan ahead; it's not a choice.

For château hotels or vineyard stays, start searching three to six months in advance, particularly if you're going in a small group or as a pair. In smaller cities where there is a shortage of lodging, even simple guesthouses and low-cost hotels fill up quickly.

Larger cities with many hotels, like Tours or Orléans, are your best bet if you're making a last-minute reservation. Be adaptable, however; in order to find anything respectable, you may need to extend your budget or make little changes to your schedule.

Events should be planned carefully since lengthy French weekends (ponts), wine festivals, and summer vacations (particularly in

August) may quickly fill up. Prior to the larger international booking platforms, local booking sites such as CléVacances, Logis Hotels, and Gîtes de France often display availability.

Also, if you're riding a bike, make sure your bike is stored properly. A hotel is not always prepared to hold your equipment overnight just because it is close to the Loire à Vélo route.

Are you going anywhere in the winter? Particularly in rural regions, a lot of vineyards and château remain shut during the off-season. Stay in locations and towns with year-round hotel operations if you're planning a winter vacation.

Local Accommodations vs. Chain Hotels: Benefits and Drawbacks

Eventually, you will have to choose between booking that cute local hotel with a quirky name and handwritten reviews or sticking with a well-known hotel brand. Here's how to balance the possibilities:

Local Accommodations (Boutique Hotels, Gîtes, and Guesthouses)

Benefits:

- More individualized service
- Usually breakfast and distinctive local accents
- Situated in picturesque or historic locations
- Closely linked to the local language and culture

Cons:

- Limited facilities or check-in hours
- Cash payment or a linguistic workaround may be necessary
- Less consistent quality if improperly screened

Ibis, Novotel, Best Western, and other chain hotels)

Advantages:

- Consistent standards
- Frequently situated close to transit hubs
- More likely to have personnel who understand English
- Simpler online reservations with reward points

Cons:

- Generic ambiance and décor
- Less personality and often a greater distance from historic districts
- Potential absence of regional cuisine or experiences

Your priorities will determine your decision. Want to delve deeply into culture? Go local. Traveling with children or putting convenience first? Chains may be more effective. It might be wise to choose a blend—spend a few nights in a vineyard and then transition to something less expensive as you visit other areas.

CHAPTER 7

DELIGHTFUL PIT STOPS EN ROUTE

Riding a bicycle across the Loire Valley is a sensory experience that offers more than simply vistas of the river and imposing châteaux. In terms of cuisine, the Loire offers something very remarkable. You're traversing a living cookbook of regional customs, local foods, and some of France's most hidden gastronomic treasures rather than just biking from one place to another.

This area offers cuisine that represents the land and the hands who produce it, whether you're in the mood for something rustic after a long ride or are looking to enjoy a three-course dinner while taking in the scenery. Eating healthily really becomes a part of your schedule. These visits are more than just breaks; they are experiences that enhance your journey, from goat cheese made exactly where you are to tarte Tatin served in its birthplace.

This chapter focuses on showing you the most delicious places in the Loire Valley and providing helpful tips along the way, such as where to locate food, what to eat, and when to take pauses like a local. As you ride through this breathtaking scenery, you'll learn just where and how to satisfy your palette.

Customary Recipes to Sample in Every Sub-Region

The Loire Valley's gastronomic variety is one of its many wonderful features. You'll see that the menus change as you go through the several départements, influenced by regional ingredients and historical trends. Eat like a native if you want to travel like one. This entails being aware of the dish that corresponds to your location on the map.

For instance, don't miss Rillettes de Tours in Touraine. A glass of Chinon red wine and crusty bread are the usual accompaniments to this slow-cooked pork spread. It's probably available in small neighborhood restaurants and butcher shops. Anjou is home to Quernons d'Ardoise, a nougatine-based confection covered in blue chocolate—yes, blue, to resemble the slate roofs of Angers.

On your way to Orléanais, you'll encounter Tarte Tatin, an inverted apple dessert with caramel that was created (by mistake) at the Hôtel Tatin in Lamotte-Beuvron. It's a must-try, particularly warm from the oven.

Look for Andouillettes de Jargeau farther east, a rustic and robust sausage dish that is a local favorite but undoubtedly an acquired taste.

Don't miss Sainte-Maure de Touraine, a goat cheese with a straw in the center (to prevent it from collapsing while age) and an ash-covered rind. In addition to being offered in markets and cheese stores, it often shows up on salads or cheeseboards at dining establishments.

And wherever you go, you can count on unabashedly rich butter, bread that crackles when you break it, and sweets that are never an afterthought. Food with character and depth has long been a source of pride for the Loire area.

Top Dining Establishments with a View

Sometimes, what you eat is just as important as what you're eating. There are many eateries in the Loire Valley where the food is as beautiful as the setting. Your supper may become a picture-perfect occasion whether you're eating by a river with the sun setting, sitting next to a château moat, or gazing out over a vineyard.

Make a reservation at Le Shaker, a riverbank restaurant with casual elegance and unrivaled sunset views over the Loire, if you're going through Amboise. After a long ride, it's ideal for a casual meal. L'Entrepotes in Chinon strikes a mix between seasonal, fresh food and rustic charm, and its garden patio seems like a private retreat.

On your way to Saumur? Both residents and bikers love L'Escargot, which is well-known for its wine selection and for the stunning nighttime views of the castle. Try La Route du Sel at Montsoreau, where you may sit outside and enjoy a front-row seat view of the Loire River.

Make reservations for lunch at Les Hauts de Loire close to Onzain for something very special. Yes, it's fancy, but bikers often visit for lunch meals that provide elegant cuisine in a casual atmosphere. In addition, it's located in a historic hunting lodge with swans and gardens all around.

Expert advice: if you're eating at a fancy restaurant, particularly during busy times (May to September), always make a reservation in advance. Hours vary more than you may think, and some even demand reservations for lunch.

Markets, Bakeries, and Cafés: Where Cyclists Refuel

Cycling increases hunger, but fortunately, there are plenty of convenient, bike-friendly refueling places in the Loire Valley. You'll want to know where to stop for a short recharge—places that appreciate a cyclist's rhythm—even if the restaurants are excellent for longer rests.

"Artisan boulanger-pâtissier." appears on the signage of boulangeries. For pain au chocolat, croissants, and freshly cooked sandwiches, these are your finest options. Towns like Blois or Tours are home to well-known brands like La Mie Câline, but the real treasures are often little, family-run bakeries nestled in back alleyways. If you want something substantial but not too heavy, try a chausson aux pommes (apple turnover) or a flan pâtissier.

Your next best buddy will be the market. You may get fresh bread, cheese, olives, fruits, and sometimes even premade crepes or rotisserie chicken at the weekly outdoor markets that are held in most towns, usually on Saturdays or Wednesdays. These are excellent for having a picnic in a château garden or along a river. Particularly well-known are the markets in places like Loches, Chinon, or Beaugency.

Small-town cafés should not be undervalued, particularly those situated in town squares or tabacs. Having a small croissant and a cup of coffee, orangina, or sparkling water can help you stay energized. You may also refill water bottles at several cafés if you ask nicely.

Several stations along the Loire à Vélo route have acknowledged the demands of cyclists by posting signs directing travelers to "accueil vélo"—bike-friendly dining and resting areas.

Seasonal Foods & Farmers' Markets

The marchés of the Loire will quickly become one of your favorite destinations if you're the kind of tourist who enjoys learning about the new and local. These markets provide you the opportunity to speak with the people who farmed or manufactured the food you're about to eat, in contrast to supermarkets or tourist stores, and they also inform you what's really in season.

You'll see Sologne strawberries, white asparagus, and the first batch of baby potatoes seasoned with regional herbs in the spring and early summer. In the fall, specialized kiosks selling wild game, pumpkins, and mushrooms from the forest of Chinon are the main attractions.

Additionally, you will encounter black bee honey, walnut oil, goat cheese matured in nearby caves, and small-batch jams that are unique to the area. Get a jar of cherry-plum confiture if you see one; it's delicious and uncommon served with cheese or on toast.

Usually, markets are open from 8 a.m. until noon. Get the finest selection and beat the crowds by arriving early. Additionally, as many businesses do not take cards, carry cash.

Inquire with locals about "marchés nocturnes" (night markets) to plan your trip. These appear throughout the summer and often include local wine vendors, street cuisine, and live music. Consider it a village celebration combined with a farmer's market, and it's a great opportunity to socialize with locals.

You will get more than just fuel if you include these culinary delights into your trip. You will learn about the leisurely, seasonal, and flavorful way of life in the Loire.

CHAPTER 8

OUTDOOR EXPERIENCES THAT GO BEYOND CYCLING

You may picture tranquil bike rides through vineyards and rural towns when you think of the Loire Valley. You're in for a surprise, however, if you're the kind of tourist who loves to switch things up and get off the saddle for a new sort of excitement. There is more to the Loire than simply riding. It's also a haven for those who like the outdoors and want diversity.

This chapter serves as your entryway to the other side of the Loire, where you may trek hidden paths behind historic châteaux, fly over vineyards in a hot air balloon, paddle down a raging river at dawn, and silently view animals in unspoiled reserves. You get a new perspective, a new rhythm, and a whole new level of connection to the valley as a result of these encounters.

Whether you're an experienced traveler or simply want to do something different in between castle visits, let's see how you may see the Loire from beyond the handlebars.

Loire River Canoeing & Kayaking

Paddling a kayak or canoe along the Loire River has an inexplicably serene quality. You are now a part of the landscape rather than just observing it. You can see nature up close in the sea. A beach, a château, or just greenery may be seen around every curve of the river, while birds sing above and little settlements appear in the distance.

You will be floating on a stream that hasn't been dammed, regulated, or unduly marketed since the Loire is France's last natural river. Respecting its unpredictable nature is also crucial. Seasons may affect water levels, and in certain locations, the current can flow swiftly. Start with a guided trip if you've never navigated a river before. From Orléans to Saumur, hundreds of outfitters provide half-day, full-day, or multi-day expeditions that include all necessary gear.

Adaptability is what you'll adore. Do you like to paddle in peace and quiet for an hour near Amboise, under the royal château? Simple. Are you interested in a full-day trip that includes wine tasting at the conclusion and stops at beaches beside rivers? That is also a possibility. Additionally, there are broad, level areas with excellent wildlife viewing and a leisurely pace for families with young children or elderly relatives.

Advice:

- Avoid crowds and wind by starting early in the morning.
- Put on non-slip shoes or sandals that may become wet.
- Pack a dry, waterproof bag for your food, maps, and phone.
- Get offline maps instead of relying on cell service when on the water.
- Inquire about the current river conditions at all times from your rental provider.

Listen to the water above anything else. Paddling it teaches you to follow its rhythm and gives it a voice of its own.

Balloon Rides in Hot Air Over Vineyards

Imagine the castle towers being brushed by the first rays of morning sunshine. From the river below, mist rose. In every direction, neat rows of grapevines like a patchwork quilt of green. And you— in a wicker basket, floating gently above it all.

There is more to a hot air balloon journey above the Loire Valley than just sightseeing. A memory is being created. Additionally, this is among the greatest locations on earth to do one if you have never done one before.

Your balloon crew will often greet you at sunrise. After that, as they fill the balloon and get ready to take off, there is a mixture of serenity and exhilaration. The movement is smoother than you may think once in the air. You are drifting, not flying. Only the occasional explosion of the flame that keeps you aloft breaks the quiet. Below, châteaux, which were magnificent from the ground, now seem as delicate ornaments, the Loire unfolds like a ribbon, and villages are scattered throughout the landscape like images from a novel.

Although the full experience (including preparation and landing) may take three or four hours, each trip lasts around an hour. The wind determines where you land, and that's part of the allure. A ride is never the same again.

Advice:

- Make reservations in advance, particularly from May to September.

- Wear layers of clothing. Even in the summer, mornings may be cold.
- You'll want to take pictures, but you don't want to drop anything, so bring a camera or phone with a wrist strap.
- When making a reservation, find out whether the excursion includes breakfast or a brief Champagne toast upon arrival.

This is one of the most romantic ways to commemorate a milestone, such as a birthday, anniversary, or proposal.

Forest Walks & Hiking Trails Close to Castles

Hiking allows you to slow down and really enjoy the Loire's countryside, while cycling transports you through its center. These walking pathways are rich in history in addition to being beautiful. Some routes are based on Roman highways from antiquity. Others meander past secret garden estates, abandoned abbeys, or megalithic stones.

Being so near to everything, while still feeling so far away, is one of the great pleasures of strolling through the Loire. Touring a château in the morning and then vanishing onto a forest path in the afternoon is possible. You don't have to pick between history and environment in locations like Chinon, Langeais, or Montsoreau since paths often go directly to the castle grounds.

If you're a committed hiker, the GR3 long-distance route passes through most of the important locations along the 1,200-kilometer Loire River. However, you are not required to dedicate a whole area. Many loops may be completed in the morning or afternoon since they are just 5–10 km long.

Well-liked locations:

- **Château de Chambord:** The national park that encircles the château has miles of designated routes through woodlands that were originally utilized for hunting by members of the royal family.
- **Montsoreau to Candes-Saint-Martin:** A stroll down a river that connects two of France's most picturesque communities.
- **Saumur's hillsides:** This is a walker's paradise with its vineyard-covered slopes and expansive river vistas.

Advice:

- Download trail maps or use hiking software like AllTrails.
- Use appropriate hiking shoes since trails may become muddy, particularly in the spring.
- For longer circuits, particularly, include food and drink.
- Bring sunblock and a hat since many of the paths are not shaded.

You gain time when you walk. It's time to listen to the birds, smell the moist land, and find a nearby shrine or ruin that you wouldn't see from a vehicle or bicycle. Don't pass up this slower viewing method.

Nature Reserves & Locations for Birdwatching

The Loire Valley has always attracted poets, painters, and nature enthusiasts for a reason.

In addition to history and wine, the terrain evokes a sense of vibrant, wild life. Some of France's most fulfilling natural experiences are hidden away from the traditional tourist route, assuming you know where to seek.

The best place to start is the Loire-Anjou-Touraine Regional Nature Park. It encompasses marshes, woodlands, and farmlands that cohabit along the river over an area of around 300,000 hectares. In addition, it is home to dozens of creatures, such as deer and beavers, more than 200 different kinds of birds, and a complex system of plants that varies with the seasons.

Bring your binoculars, birdwatchers. The river serves as a significant migratory route from spring to fall. If you're fortunate, you may see black storks, ospreys, egrets, and herons. Great view opportunities are provided by observation towers close to Candes-Saint-Martin and the meeting point of the Vienne and Loire rivers.

Some reserves, particularly in the spring and summer, provide classes or guided hikes. They are managed by local environmentalists who really care about the land, thus they are not touristic. This might be a fantastic approach to get children enthused about nature while you're traveling with them.

Advice:

- Bring insect repellent during the warmer months since mosquitoes are frequent near wetlands.
- Mornings and evenings are the ideal times to see animals.

- Be patient and walk gently since many animals avoid loud noises.
- During mating seasons, entrance to certain sites is limited; please heed warnings and instructions.

These areas provide a welcome reset, even if you're not a die-hard nature lover. A peaceful hour by the river or among the trees after the bustle of marketplaces, castles, and eateries serves as a reminder of why this valley has always been cherished, not just for the things that people have constructed but also for the things that nature has kept.

CHAPTER 9

LOCAL LIFE, LANGUAGE HINTS, AND CULTURAL ETIQUETTE

The Loire Valley is home to rich customs, ageless rural rhythms, and a local culture that values respect and curiosity in addition to châteaux and vineyards. Beyond just sightseeing, you may enhance your trip by learning about the customs, manners, and everyday life of the area. This chapter is your go-to travel guide if you want to fit in rather than stick out.

Your ability to understand local traditions makes a tremendous difference, whether you're purchasing a croissant at a boulangerie, chatting with a winemaker, or exploring a languid Sunday market. Additionally, knowing the rhythm of French everyday life and a few useful words may open doors (both literally and figuratively) if you're riding through smaller towns where English isn't generally spoken. Consider this chapter to be your cultural decoder ring, guiding you into the Loire Valley rather than merely to it.

From polite welcomes to knowing when not to expect anything to be open, let's take you through it all. You'll leave feeling more prepared, self-assured, and incredibly connected to the people and locations that make this region of France so unique.

Essential French Words for Passengers

You're not alone if you're concerned about the language barrier, but you don't have to speak it well to travel with confidence in the Loire

Valley. In reality, many people will be kind, understanding, and even thrilled by your effort if you know a few essential words and have a positive attitude.

Although bonjour and merci are fundamental, we'll go beyond them in this part and concentrate on the words that will be most helpful to you as a traveler. You'll discover how to:

- Get directions to the closest château, hire a bike, or go wine tasting
- Place a courteous order at a café or restaurant
- Manage bookings and hotel check-ins
- Handle medical inquiries and crises

To make your French seem more natural, even if you're only stating je ne parle pas français très bien (I don't speak French very well), you'll also learn some pronunciation suggestions. With the help of these resources, you will be able to feel at ease when navigating everything from a ticket machine to a bakery counter.

Here, the emphasis is on situational language rather than simply words, so you're never taken by surprise in real-life situations. You'll be prepared to manage it with elegance whether you're eating at a restaurant with a Michelin star or purchasing strawberries from a market stall.

How to Respectfully Engage Locals

The Loire Valley is no exception to France's renowned etiquette. Don't worry, however; being thoughtful is more important than being formal. Little acts of civility have a big impact.

This section provides you with concise, useful advice on how to avoid blunders and win over the locals:

- Vous should always be used first, as opposed to tu.
- How to act during a wine tasting or castle tour (including what not to do)
- Why you should always say "Bonjour" when you enter a store and "Au revoir" when you exit
- Tipping traditions in guided tours, taxis, and restaurants
- How to interpret nonverbal clues and tone of voice
- The value of waiting your time in culture and the reasons why hurrying might be seen as impolite

Additionally, you'll learn how to modify your conduct according to the situation, whether you're in a little town like Candes-Saint-Martin or a busy metropolis like Tours. The secret is to be patient, humble, and respectful of the local way of life. You will often get warm, inquisitive treatment in return.

Holiday Closures, Strikes, and Opening Hours

A handmade fermé exceptionnellement (exceptionally closed) sign on the door might ruin your carefully planned day. That's simply a part of traveling in France, particularly when visiting smaller cities or as the seasons change.

With insider information that isn't always available online, this part gets you ready for real-world situations:

- When restaurants really open and why it matters to arrive at noon sharp
- The "sacred" midday shutdown hour for many stores and services, which is between 12 and 2 PM
- Why Sundays might seem even more like ghost towns than Mondays
- How transportation, eating, and sightseeing are impacted by regional and national holidays such as Bastille Day, Assumption Day, and municipal festivals
- How to locate trustworthy information and backup plans in the event that a rail strike or protest interrupts your schedule

Not only can planning around these local realities help you avoid annoyance, but it also brings you closer to the organic rhythm of French living. You may prevent empty streets, closed doors, and needless tension by being adaptable and modifying your expectations.

Local Customs & Festival Features

Beyond the castles and wine, the Loire Valley is teeming with customs, some of which have been maintained for generations and others that have been revitalized by contemporary fervor. These regional traditions provide windows into the spirit of the area, whether it's a silent religious procession, a wine harvest fête, or a medieval reenactment.

In this part, you will go through the following seasons:

- Historic festivals like the Fête Jeanne d'Arc in Orléans or the Festival des Jardins in Chaumont-sur-Loire

- Small-town customs like outdoor concerts, brocantes (vintage markets), and artisan fairs
- Catholic feast days and their impact on public life, even if you're not religious
- The Vendanges (grape harvest) celebrations in Anjou and Touraine
- When and where to locate culinary events honoring regional wine, cheese, or mushrooms

We'll assist you in scheduling your visit to coincide with the most noteworthy occasions and provide guidance on how to participate politely. You will feel more than simply a spectator, whether you are applauding a knight in costume or clapping along with a folk band at a winery celebration.

It's not just about viewing a parade; you'll also discover the more profound backstories of these festivities, so you'll know why They are important to the community.

CHAPTER 10

INSIGHTFUL TRAVEL ADVICE & COMMON ERRORS TO AVOID

You're doing something well if your planning has progressed this far or if you're already in the Loire Valley. However, little nuances have the potential to trip up even the most experienced travelers. This chapter fills that need. Think of it as your defense against tension, lost time, and the post-trip "I wish I'd known" regrets that many tourists have.

This chapter provides really useful tips to help you make the most of your stay in France without falling into the typical pitfalls, regardless of whether you're a first-time traveler or an experienced traveler hoping to explore the country more. Every tip offered here is intended to provide you confidence and peace of mind while you travel, from avoiding overscheduling to understanding which applications may really benefit you.

You won't find anything ambiguous or filler-filled here, and I won't bombard you with theory or general counsel. Rather, you'll get straightforward, practical advice based on actual circumstances that tourists like you deal with on a daily basis. Traveling smarter is the goal here, not simply better travel. Because you may appreciate the Loire Valley in its most authentic form—completely, freely, and joyfully—when you know what to avoid and how to get ready.

The Top Ten Rookie Errors (and How to Avoid Them)

Even experienced visitors fall into traps while visiting the Loire Valley. Although the area is dispersed, pleasantly leisurely, and full of sights, it may also be logistically challenging if you're not sure what to anticipate. I'll go over 10 of the most typical beginner errors in this part, along with—and maybe more importantly—how to prevent them.

Here is a preview of the topics we will cover:

- Not learning basic French greetings or etiquette, which results in awkward or cold encounters
- Trying to fit too much into one day by underestimating travel times between villages or castles

- Assuming every château is open daily and not booking tickets in advance for popular spots like Château de Chambord or Chenonceau
- Being caught off guard by midday closures in small towns
- Selecting lodgings that are far from important cycling routes or transportation links
- Not accounting for the weather while organizing outside activities, particularly in the spring or autumn
- I'm assuming that every winery accepts walk-ins, even if many need appointments.
- Overpacking or failing to prepare appropriately for unexpected weather changes

- Relying too much on ride-sharing apps or assuming that taxis would be easily accessible in remote places
- Being under the impression that you can "wing it" during peak months like July and August

Every error has a practical remedy, such as a downloaded program, a reservation technique, or just a shift in perspective. Learning from the errors of others allows you to have a more enjoyable and easy path.

How to Steer Clear of Tourist Pitfalls

The Loire Valley isn't Paris; it's less touristy, less marketed, and often seems surprisingly genuine. However, it doesn't imply that certain tourist traps or expensive diversions aren't present close to the more well-known locations. I'll show you how to recognize them—and avoid them—in this part so you can invest your time and money where it matters most.

You will discover:

- Why "wine tastings" on the main road could not really represent the quality or character of the area
- How to spot expensive restaurants close to big châteaux and where to discover genuine alternatives nearby
- How to avoid overspending on subpar souvenirs that aren't produced locally
- When guided tours are worthwhile—and when you're better off traveling alone with a self-directed app or booklet

- How to prioritize really fulfilling events and what to forgo if you're pressed for time
- How to avoid crowded timeslots by modifying your schedule or route
- When internet evaluations might be misleading (and how to look between the lines)
- Why purchasing "experience packages" without doing any research might result in higher costs and worse quality

Instead of just telling you to "don't do this," I'll provide you with compelling alternatives—better solutions that allow you to experience the Loire Valley more authentically and often at a lower cost. Because being a wise traveler involves recognizing where the real fun is, not avoiding it.

Essentials for Safety, Health, and Travel Insurance

Although traveling is an adventure, there are unknowns involved. On your rental bike, you can acquire a flat tire. Your flight may be canceled. Or maybe you consume something that doesn't suit you. For this reason, basic health preparation, safety knowledge, and travel insurance are for smart travelers, not just anxious ones.

In this part, I will guide you:

- The kinds of travel insurance that are very important for visitors to the Loire Valley, such as medical coverage, trip interruption, and coverage for equipment like bike rentals

- How to locate local pharmacies or hospitals in the event of an accident (yes, even in remote locations)
- How to get emergency treatment in France and the necessary paperwork
- Safety advice for bikers, particularly while commuting on constrained routes with cars
- Keeping oneself secure while traveling alone or exploring new places
- A basic travel health kit should include the following items, which you may readily get locally if necessary
- How to ask for what you need and what is accessible without a prescription in France's drugstore system
- Particular attention if you suffer from chronic illnesses, allergies, or mobility problems

Being prepared to adjust so that a little setback doesn't spoil your vacation is what it means to plan for safety, not to assume the worst. Knowing that you've taken care of everything will make you feel more at ease and in the moment.

Keeping in Touch: Apps, Wi-Fi, and SIM Cards

Traveling properly doesn't need you to be tied to your computer, but having the appropriate digital tools may help a lot, particularly in places like the Loire Valley where public transportation is scarce and signs may be in French. In this part, I'll help you remain connected in a sensible, cost-effective manner.

Here's what we'll cover:

- Where to find free and dependable Wi-Fi (and where not to rely on it)
- The best SIM card options for travelers, including local providers like Orange Holiday or Bouygues, and where to get them upon arrival
- Advice on how to use eSIMs if your phone supports them—so you're connected before you even land
- Which travel apps are worth downloading for offline navigation, maps, bookings for château, translation, and cycling routes
- Tips for conserving data and avoiding unexpected roaming fees
- How to call French numbers, including emergency contacts or restaurant reservations
- Backup methods if your phone fails or goes stolen (including utilizing hotel

business cards, paper maps, and written reservations)

This is about utilizing technology to enhance your trip, not to detract from it. It is not about always being connected. With the appropriate arrangement, you'll be able to wander freely without always worrying about getting lost, missing a booking, or being out of contact.

CONCLUSION

As you complete this tour, I would like to express my gratitude for entrusting you with your exploration of the Loire Valley. I hope this book has given you clarity, confidence, and delight, whether you're already thinking back on the castles, wine, and riverbank towns, or you're still organizing the ideal vacation.

This book was thoughtfully crafted, with each page based on genuine traveler requirements and candid local knowledge. My intention has always been to help you travel more intelligently, deeply, and meaningfully—not merely to provide you with a list of locations to visit.

I would very appreciate it if you could take a time to give a review if this guide helped you make better decisions, reduce stress, or find something you would have missed otherwise. To help other travelers choose if this is the perfect book for them, even a few sentences may make a big difference. Your comments serve as a compass for the next reader, not only for me.

And it's not farewell.

I'm Aarav Nath Wayfarer, and I've dedicated my life to writing travel guides that are sincere, realistic, and compassionate. Check out my other titles whether you're planning a trip or are just daydreaming about your next vacation. Based on actual travel experiences and inquiries from tourists just like you, I'm always adding new content.

In the meanwhile, continue to travel sensibly, explore fearlessly, and make lifelong experiences.

Always travel safely.

The author of your adventure across the Loire Valley and many more to come is *Aarav Nath Wayfarer*.

Printed in Dunstable, United Kingdom